"[E]ach created thing is an indispensable factor of the great whole." —GWC

George Washington CARVER

Tonya Bolden

Published in Association with The Field Museum, Chicago

ABRAMS BOOKS FOR YOUNG READERS
NEW YORK

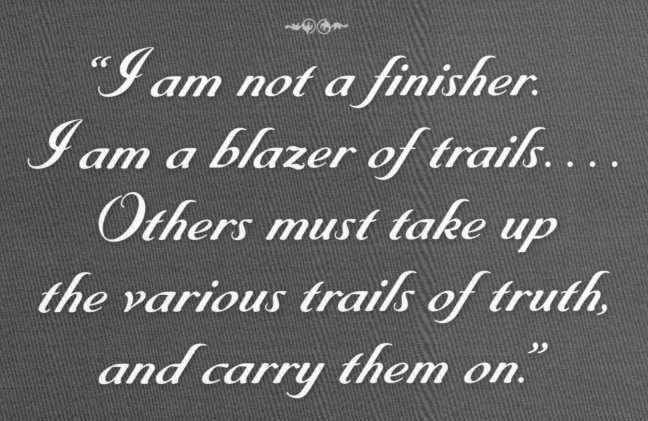

"*I am not a finisher.
I am a blazer of trails. . . .
Others must take up
the various trails of truth,
and carry them on.*"

So said an ailing, elderly George Washington Carver,
a soul ever in awe of nature—and an astonishment
himself, given his tragic beginnings.

OPPOSITE PAGE: Carver called his laboratory "God's little workshop."

3

George's early home may have looked similar to this one.

He was born in Missouri's Ozarks region, near the frontier town of Diamond Grove, during the Civil War (1861–65). Little is known about his father, but his mother was a young woman named Mary. Along with her children, she was enslaved on Moses and Susan Carver's farm.

George was a baby and his brother, Jim, about six when criminals invaded the farm. Stymied in their hope of finding and stealing hidden gold, the men galloped off on horseback with George and his mother instead. The tracker whom Moses Carver sent to their rescue returned with the baby only (and received a prized horse in reward). Not long after that, the Civil War, and later slavery, were over.

George and Jim, never to see their mother again, were raised by the Carvers, with George suffering bad colds, whooping cough, and bouts of another respiratory ailment, the croup. He was also slow to walk. Talking came late too. When he finally spoke, he had a stammer and a squeaky voice.

Susan and Moses Carver, both of German descent, were opposed to slavery. Some suggest that George's mother was a mercy purchase, but it is unclear why she was not therefore immediately freed.

Life with "Uncle Mose" and "Aunt Sue," as the brothers called their guardians, was free from worries about food, shelter, and such, but there were cows to milk; cattle to graze; corn and other crops to sow and reap; a vegetable garden to seed and weed; horses to water and feed; deer and other game to hunt; plus apple, hazelnut, and other fruit- and nut-bearing trees and bushes to pick.

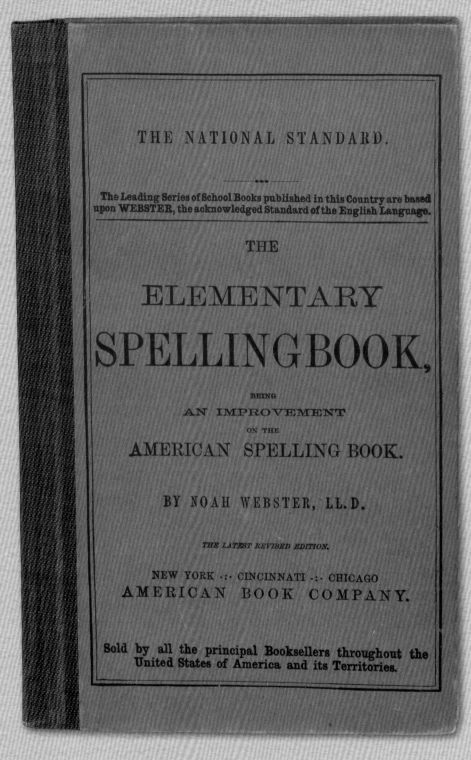

THE NATIONAL STANDARD.

•••

The Leading Series of School Books published in this Country are based upon WEBSTER, the acknowledged Standard of the English Language.

THE

ELEMENTARY

SPELLING BOOK,

BEING

AN IMPROVEMENT

ON THE

AMERICAN SPELLING BOOK.

BY NOAH WEBSTER, LL.D.

THE LATEST REVISED EDITION.

NEW YORK ·:· CINCINNATI ·:· CHICAGO
AMERICAN BOOK COMPANY.

Sold by all the principal Booksellers throughout the United States of America and its Territories.

George used a book like this one to learn to read and write.

Jim plowed, chopped wood, and did other sweat-and-muscle work. Little brother George was too sickly for that, but he could churn butter, drop corn kernels into furrows, collect eggs from the chicken coop, and groom the horses and give them oats. Picking the gems from the limbs of persimmon trees was more pleasure than chore. George loved that fruit.

The kid was a whiz as Aunt Sue's housework helper and a crackerjack at handicrafts, from carving to crocheting. When he wanted to knit, he made needles from turkey feathers. Such ingenuity was standard for country folk. They looked to the natural world for much more than the makings of meals.

The slate that George used as a child.

Uncle Mose tanned deerskin for shoes and sundry leather goods. Aunt Sue made clothing with wool sheared from their sheep and flax grown in their fields. Boiled bark of oak, chestnut, and hickory trees became black, brown, and yellow dyes.

To heal a wound, the Carvers used leaves of the weed plantain; to soothe a cough, the herb tansy combined with honey from their beehives. Moreover, nothing went to waste, from table scraps (food for livestock) to fireplace ashes (for soap making).

George made excellent use of a hand-me-down spelling book. The more he studied, the more it hurt that the closest school (in Locust Grove) was for white children only.

"I wanted to know the name of every stone and flower and insect and bird and beast. I wanted to know where it got its colors, where it got its life."
—GWC

During his rambles, George probably came upon scenes like this (a depiction of Hinkson Creek in central Missouri).

OPPOSITE PAGE:
A watercolor landscape by George. Date unknown.

SCENE ON THE HINKSON, UNIVERSITY OF MISSOURI, COLUMBIA.

Exploring the woods was George's perpetual pick-me-up, his best adventure, his bliss. Wandering. Wondering. Watching for wonder. Whistling along to birdsong. All the while, he wanted to know the "why" of everything, from the varieties of rain to the beauty of begonias, believing that there was a God and that all of nature was God's creation.

When out in the woods, whether listening to chipmunk chatter, gazing at grass-hoppers, tiptoeing around toadstools, or marveling at milkweed, the boy felt closest to his God, whom he came to call the Great Creator.

George's love of nature led to a rock collection in a corner of the Carver cabin; a pen for pet frogs outside; and farther away, a garden he kept secret for fear of scorn. It was "considered foolishness," he later recalled, for a boy to "waste time on flowers." That didn't hold true in his case—not after he revived one woman's ferns, then made another neighbor's rosebushes robust. Whatever was needed—more watering, less watering, additional sand in the soil, a better site in the sun—George naturally knew what to do. People called him "the Plant Doctor."

His peek at paintings in a neighbor's parlor moved him to make art. He had no canvas, no paintbrushes, and no paint. But he did have stones, wood, and other found things on which to compose shapes. Bunched-together twigs became brushes. For colors, he boiled bark and juiced berries.

"Carver's George," as he was called, and as he called himself, added art to the list of things about which he longed to know more. When he was around twelve, he made up his mind to move to nearby Neosho, a town with a school for blacks.

He left home with the Carvers' blessing, Jim's good-luck wishes, and his belongings in a bandanna.

In Neosho, George found favor with Andrew and Mariah Watkins, for whom he did chores in exchange for room and board. His duties ranged from housework to helping the missus hunt for plants and herbs with healing powers, crucial for the people doctoring she did.

"Aunt Mariah" quickly divined the power of his mind. "You must learn all you can and then go out into the world and give your learning back to our people that's so starving for a little learning," she urged, no doubt thinking mainly of survivors of slavery. She also told him to stop calling himself "Carver's George," for he was no one's property.

Within a year, the boy learned all that he could at the Neosho school. As "George Carver," he moved on.

aunt mariah's home.

school

Carver's drawing of the Watkins home and the one-room school, Lincoln, he attended. Date unknown.

OPPOSITE PAGE: Mariah Watkins. This midwife and healer was a member of the local African Methodist Episcopal church, which George attended while living with her and her husband, a gardener and Mr. Fix-It. This photograph was taken around that time.

Carver at age thirteen or so. Top contenders for his birth are the summer of 1864 and the spring of 1865. His brother (b. 1859) would die of smallpox as a young man. Carver later in life referred to "sisters," but this is the only reference we have to them.

OPPOSITE PAGE:
A typical sod house. Carver's was fourteen square feet. While homesteading near Beeler, Kansas, he joined a literary society and played the accordion at socials.

George Carver kicked around Kansas for about ten years, doing domestic work mostly. He added to his formal education in snatches, finally finishing high school in 1885, in Minneapolis, Kansas. That's where he adopted the middle initial "W." (Another George Carver in town resulted in mail mix-ups.) When he was asked if the "W" stood for "Washington," after America's first president, this wanderer's attitude was, Why not?

That why-not spirit prompted him to apply to Highland University in northeast Kansas. When accepted by mail, he rejoiced, but this lift was short-lived.

"We take Indians here, but no Negroes," a Highland official told him when he showed up to enroll. Shortly after that, Carver became a homesteader in western Kansas, sod house and all.

Life on the plains was full of delights, from yucca plants and turkey-foot grass to the northern lights. What's more, Carver met a woman happy to give him art lessons and pointers on his newfound love, poetry.

None of this outweighed the hardships, though, such as rainless late-spring days and a winter's brutal blizzard. By 1888, Carver had had enough of homesteading. He wound up in Winterset, Iowa, where he worked as a cook in a hotel. Yet again, he met a white couple, John and Helen Milholland, who took a shine to his mind. With their encouragement, he enrolled in Simpson College, in Indianola, Iowa. This school didn't have a no-blacks policy.

Carver in an art class at Simpson College.

Carver's art teacher, Etta May Budd, with her family. She is flanked by her parents, Joseph and Sarah. Behind them, brother Allen.

When Carver entered Simpson in September 1890, he hoped to become a professional painter, but new plans began to take shape after his art teacher, Etta May Budd, saw some of the plant doctoring he did in his spare time. Budd urged him to do more about his passion for nature than paint plants. She convinced him to transfer to a college in Ames, Iowa, where her father, Joseph Budd, was a professor of horticulture (the art and science of raising plants and flowers). Impressed with some of Carver's work, Professor Budd was eager to have him as a student.

Carver poses with his oil on linen *Yucca and Cactus*, inspired by his homesteading days. Thanks to encouragement and funds from fellow students, he entered this painting in an art show in Cedar Rapids, Iowa, in late 1892. *Yucca and Cactus* was among artwork chosen to represent the Hawkeye State at the 1893 world's fair in Chicago. It received an honorable mention.

Carver (back row) in Creamery Operators class, circa 1894, at what is now Iowa State University, where he was its first black student and professor. Carver's extracurricular activities included membership in the German and art clubs and playing the guitar.

At Iowa Agricultural College and Model Farm, Carver excelled in horticulture as well as botany (the study of plant life). In class after class, he made his professors proud, especially Louis Pammel, an expert in mycology (the study of fungi such as mushrooms) and a pioneer in ecology (the study of the interrelatedness of the vegetable, mineral, and animal worlds). Professor Pammel wanted Carver to add a master's to his bachelor's degree (which he earned in 1894). When Carver agreed, the college made him an assistant professor of botany.

While Carver was moving from strength to strength in Iowa, Booker T. Washington, principal of a school for blacks in Tuskegee, Alabama, was determined to lure him away.

Washington's March 1896 letter to Carver began: "Tuskegee Institute seeks to provide education—a means for survival to those who attend. Our students are poor, often starving. They travel miles of torn roads, across years of poverty. We teach them to read and write, but words cannot fill stomachs. They need to learn how to plant and harvest crops." Carver would have "the challenge of bringing people from degradation, poverty and waste" to more fruitful lives. Washington wanted him to design and run the agricultural department, teach courses, and do research.

Washington's letter echoed Mariah Watkins's words: *You must learn all you can and then go out into the world and give your learning back to our people.*

Carver was already considering an offer from another black school, Alcorn Agricultural and Mechanical College in Mississippi, but Tuskegee had an advantage: Carver greatly admired Washington. At either place, Carver would be leaving his comfort zone. He had spent most of his life among whites. He had never lived in the Deep South, which was generally a more oppressive place for blacks—and even more so when the U.S. Supreme Court legalized segregation in the case *Plessy v. Ferguson*. The ruling was handed down in mid-May 1896. Carver had committed to Tuskegee by then. There was no turning back.

In early October 1896, having earned his master's degree, he headed south, bearing boxes of prized plants, fungi, and rocks; parcels of his paintings; and a great going-away gift from folks in Iowa: a microscope.

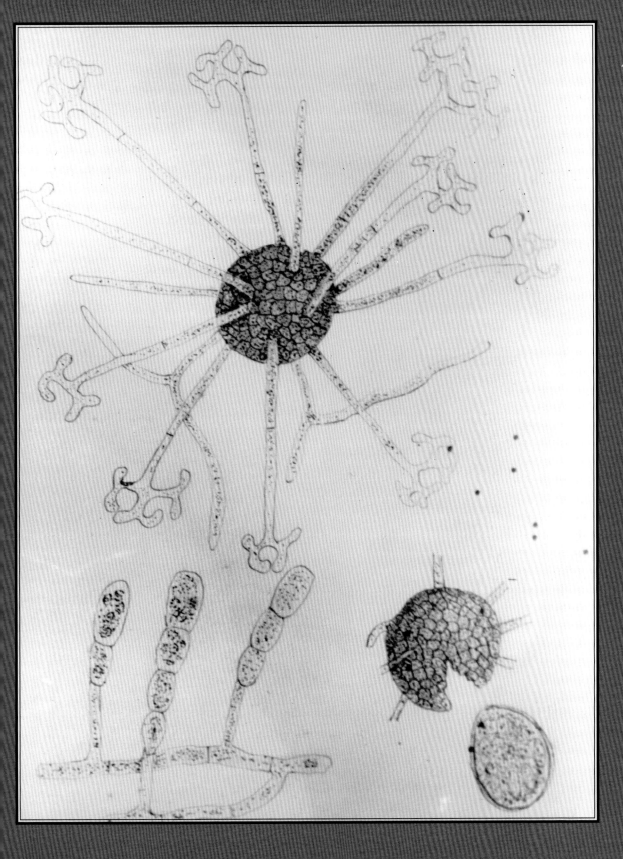

A scientific drawing made by Carver while he was at Iowa, where he contributed about 1,500 fungi to the school's herbarium and was especially gifted at crossbreeding and grafting plants. His writings include "Plants as Modified by Man" (bachelor's thesis) and the articles "Grafting the Cacti" and "Best Ferns for the North and Northwest."

OPPOSITE PAGE: The microscope Carver took with him to Tuskegee.

What Carver saw of southeast Alabama from the train and during the horsedrawn carriage ride from the depot to Tuskegee's campus was heartbreaking:

[T]he acres of cotton, nothing but cotton. . . . The scraggly cotton grew close up to the cabin doors; a few lonesome collards, the only sign of vegetables; stunted cattle, boney mules; fields and hillsides cracked and scarred with gullies and deep ruts. . . . Not much evidence of scientific farming anywhere. Everything looked hungry: the land, the cotton, the cattle, and the people.

At the time Carver arrived at Tuskegee, sharecroppers were made by the local landowners to grow cotton, a money-maker (for the landowners), rather than cultivate food and raise livestock. Carver met many people subsisting on diets heavy on fatback and molasses and plagued by skin rashes, minds less than lively, and other symptoms of pellagra, a deficiency of the vitamin niacin, found in poultry, whole grains, and green vegetables, among other foods.

OPPOSITE PAGE: The 1881 beginnings of what became the coed teacher-training and vocational school Tuskegee Normal and Industrial Institute (now Tuskegee University).

Decades of cultivating cotton, cotton, cotton had sapped the soil's vitality, leaving it in a state of near starvation. Most of the farmers were sharecroppers.

Tuskegee Institute was hungry too. Many of its two thousand acres were swampland. Many instructors held classes in shacks, as would Carver until the agricultural building became a brick-and-mortar reality. There was nothing about the campus for the artist in Carver to adore.

"The soil here is not good. Do you think grass would grow?" Washington asked Carver shortly after he settled in.

"I'll do what I can."

21

Carver passing by rows of corn at the Experiment Station, where he tested the viability of different crops and varieties of no-cost organic fertilizer in his stated mission of helping "the man farthest down," as he and others called the poor.

OPPOSITE PAGE: Carver, a true believer in hands-on education, shows students cow and calf skeletons assembled by two biology students. He also took botany students on nature hikes and specimen hunts.

Making grass grow was a metaphor for Carver's workload. Along with creating an agricultural course of study, teaching, and research, he was in charge of the school's orchard, beehives, poultry, livestock, dairy, and two farms. Supervising campus landscaping and grounds maintenance was also among his duties. So was improving the school's outreach programs to local farmers. When state funds came through for an agricultural Experiment Station in early 1897, Carver would manage that twenty-acre plot too.

For research, Carver's only laboratory equipment was his microscope. He was disappointed, but he didn't despair. Using bottles and jars as beakers and Bunsen burners; small bowls and teacups as containers; a flatiron for grinding; reeds as pipettes; and old pots and pans as this and that, Carver analyzed soil, plants, and more to study his new surroundings and come up with cures for at least some of what caused the heartbreaking hunger.

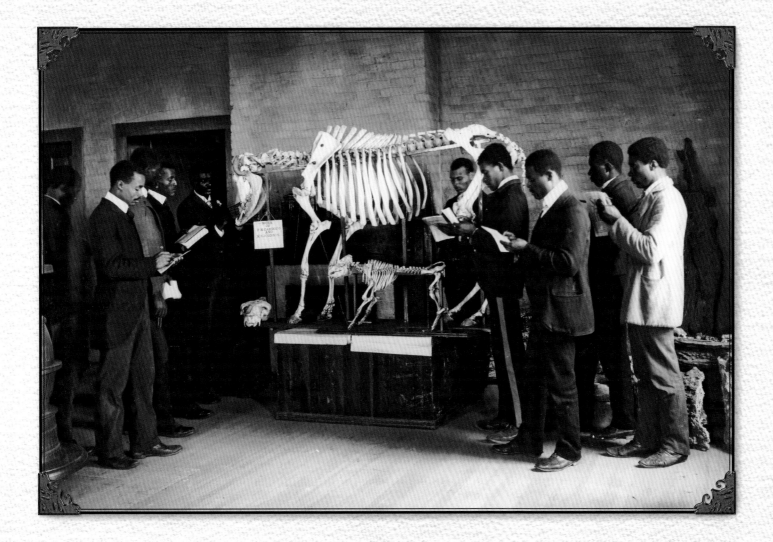

Regard nature. Revere nature. Respect nature. This was Carver's message, and spreading it was how he helped.

Had he possessed a magic wand, he would have waved away the subjugation of black folks that was at the root of so much of the hunger. If he had had the temperament of a Frederick Douglass or an Ida B. Wells, he might have packed away that microscope and raised rallies for equality of opportunity and against night riders and lynch mobs.

Carver was no magician, no Douglass, no Wells. He was his own unique self with much to offer flowing from his innate and studied insights into nature's ways and gifts.

A drawing of *Mentzelia ornata*, or prairie lily, by Carver.

Whether teaching subjects such as botany and chemistry or techniques such as deep plowing and crop rotation, Carver sought to instill in his students the belief that it was in their best interest to treasure nature and not just take from it.

"The farmer whose soil produces less every year, is unkind to it in some way," he stated in *The Negro Farmer*, a Tuskegee-based journal. Those who were unkind to the soil—"soil robbers," he called them—were ultimately harming themselves. The sicker the soil, the less potent and plentiful the produce that farmers brought to market and into their own homes.

Carver touted a way that farmers could renew their bodies and the earth: by planting crops largely ignored in the South, including sweet potatoes, which many call yams; cowpeas, also known as black-eyed peas; and goobers, another name for peanuts. All are rich in vitamins and minerals, and all return nutrients to the soil as they grow.

He shared his gospel of earth-care-as-self-care with farmers he met during

Tuskegee's Jesup Agricultural Wagon, built by students, was named after its first benefactor, the wealthy white New Yorker Morris Ketchum Jesup. Later, the wagon was replaced by a truck.

BELOW: This ad urges people to bring samples of their sick soil and troubled trees, promising that Carver will provide the remedies, for "he is the man to answer."

GET READY
FOR THE
Farmers' Picnic
WHICH WILL BE HELD AT
Mt. Pleasant Church, One Mile South of Mathews,
Saturday, July 15th, 1905.

A GRAND SUBJECT FOR DEBATE,
"IS IT OUR DUTY TO EDUCATE OUR CHILDREN?"
This subject will be discussed by some of our ablest people, among whom are, Prof. John A. Wilson, of Montgomery, Ala.; Rev. Shepherd Scott, of Mamie, Ala.; Prof. Augustus Elmore, of Mathews, Ala.; Prof. Geo. W. Carver, of Tuskegee, Ala.; Mr. William Hinson, of Cecil, Ala.

ALL ARE INVITED TO ATTEND.
Prof. Geo. W. Carver is one of the best educated men in our colored race. If your soil don't produce crops well bring some with you and he will tell you the reason why. Some of your fruit trees are failing to bear as they should, break off a small branch and bring it with you, and you will be told the cause. Any question on any kind of plant or any kind of soil you are at liberty to ask him: he is the man to answer. Don't miss this Grand Picnic. Come and be with us, and feast on the many delicacies we are going to have. Bring tables if desired. Flying Jennies, Watermelon Wagons, etc. Taxes on Tables 25c., Flying Jennies $2.00, Watermelon wagons 15c.

FRANK HINSON, President
ARTHUR BURKE, Secretary.

walks, in churches, and at Tuskegee Institute's outreach programs. These included a yearly Farmers' Conference. There was also a monthly Farmers' Institute, which frequently featured cooking demonstrations by students and lessons on meal planning, along with workshops on agriculture.

For farmers unable to attend on-campus offerings, Tuskegee's movable school, the Jesup Agricultural Wagon, was a real boon. Outfitted with displays and equipment, the wagon took Carver's learning out to the people.

By HYMAN

The "waste not, want not" principle Carver had learned as a child was key to being a good steward of the good earth, he believed. To students, to farmers—to anyone who would listen—he stressed that the Great Creator was not the author of waste. "Garbage" was most always a failure of insight and ingenuity.

Why spend money on chemical fertilizer if you have barnyard manure? No barnyard animals? Make compost heaps: piles of vegetable peelings, table scraps, leaves, grass, rags, and other matter that rotted relatively quickly and recycled itself into a breeding ground for new life.

"Save everything. From what you have make what you want," Carver charged. Using clay to make house paint—as he saw a local woman do—was a fine example. He urged others to do likewise. A home adorned was not a luxury but nourishment for the soul—and not impossible for the poor with a little resourcefulness. To this end, he also gave away starter seeds for flower gardens.

A cornhusk horse collar like this was displayed at Tuskegee's 1906 Farmers' Conference.

OPPOSITE PAGE: Tuskegee-grown cabbage

A sampling of Carver's bulletins. *Nature's Garden for Victory and Peace* (second from left, top) was issued during World War II, a time of food shortages. The bulletin offers information on the nutritional and medicinal value of milkweed, dandelions, oxeye daisies, and other plants commonly discounted as useless weeds.

OPPOSITE PAGE:
The Tuskegee campus, circa 1916.

Carver presented many of his lessons for better living in bulletins, written simply so that the average person could digest the information easily and convey it ably to people who couldn't read. Some of these pamphlets zeroed in on an aspect of agriculture, such as how to increase crop yield; others, on making the most of a harvest—for example, Bulletin 26: *When, What, and How to Can and Preserve Fruits and Vegetables in the Home.*

A few months after that publication came off the press, Carver was in mourning like everyone else at Tuskegee Institute. Booker T. Washington had died on November 14, 1915.

Washington and Carver's relationship had become rocky. Carver had infuriated Washington with his lackadaisical ways when it came to paperwork and other administrative duties. Washington had frustrated Carver with frequent denials of more funds for his work. Still, the two men had respected each other. They were kindred spirits in their commitment to uplifting the downtrodden.

Before Washington died, he had seen Carver make grass and so much else grow at Tuskegee. By this time, Carver had a better lab and his workload was lighter. Another man was running the agricultural department. Carver's title was now director of research, and he longed to spend even more time in his lab.

Tuskegee's new chief, Robert Moton, allowed Carver to limit his classroom time to summer courses for teachers and freed him from managing the Experiment Station. Moton wasn't just being kind. Carver had become a very in-demand speaker, bringing positive publicity to the school. Moton wanted to keep him happy.

"Tuskegee Normal and Industrial Institute."

In Carver's presentations at conferences, county fairs, schools, and other venues in Alabama and beyond, he dazzled audiences with his displays of manifold uses for agricultural products, chiefly the sweet potato and the peanut.

Carver had tested different ways of cooking sweet potatoes (baking, steaming, boiling, frying) and various sweet potato recipes (including muffins, doughnuts, and croquettes). Sugar, starch, flour, vinegar, molasses, and ink are among the dozens of products he knew could be made from parts of the sweet potato, root to vine. With the

FRESH

ROASTED

LEFT: *Arachis hypogaea* is the peanut's scientific name. Only after the boll weevil blighted Alabama cotton fields in 1915 did the state's peanut farming soar.

ABOVE: *Ipomoea batatas* is the scientific name for the sweet potato, a member of the morning glory family.

OPPOSITE PAGE: Farmers harvesting peanuts.

peanut, he promoted not dozens but hundreds of by-products. As a result, some called Carver "the Wizard of Tuskegee"; others, "the Wizard of the Goober and the Yam." The tag that would stick: "the Peanut Man."

"You'd think I knew nothing about anything but peanuts and sweet potatoes," Carver lamented late in life. When a reporter asked if his peanut research was his crowning glory, Carver replied, "No," adding, "but it has been featured more than my other work."

Carver was partly to blame. He rarely said no when asked to advise peanut farmers, manufacturers, and others in the peanut industry. Sure, he wanted to be helpful (always refusing to charge for his consultations), but he also enjoyed the attention. He reaped a bumper crop of that after his appearance before a U.S. House of Representatives committee on January 21, 1921.

The issue before the committee was whether to levy a heavy tax on peanuts from abroad. The United Peanut Growers' Association paid for Carver's trip to the capital to speak on the boundless possibilities of the peanut and thus the potential prosperity for the American peanut industry if foreign competition was beat back. Carver had ten minutes to make his case.

Peanut-derived flour, meal, and cereals were some of the first things he showcased, along with nonfoods such as dyes—"ranging from black to orange yellow"—from peanut skins. The committee became so riveted that its chairman wound up telling Carver, "Your time is unlimited."

"In dirt is life." —GWC

From such dirt Carver made not only whitewash but also pottery, as well as paints for his "brushwork," as he called his painting.

OPPOSITE PAGE: Two bottles of peanuts, a bottle of a peanut-derived animal feed, and some of Carver's commercial peanut products: a bar of soap (front); peanut oil (center); peanut protein and peanut mill (back row, left to right). The two tall bottles are Penol, for respiratory ailments.

The rest of Carver's show-and-tell included candies, milk, ice cream, fruit punches, oils, instant coffee, and face cream produced from peanuts. He spoke of how soft cheeses and mock meats could be made with peanut curds. "We are going to use less and less meat just as soon as science touches these various vegetable products, and teaches us how to use them," he predicted.

The U.S. peanut industry got its protective tariff. The publicity around Carver's testimony sealed his fate as the Peanut Man. Exaggerations about his work would abound, with people crediting him with other people's discoveries, most notably the invention of peanut butter.

Carver became a hostage to the hype; he didn't have it in him to tell people to stop calling him the Peanut Man. He could only hope that the Peanut Man propaganda would be an asset when he decided to market plant-derived products. Making mounds of money wasn't his motivation, but rather, advancing the cause of wise, efficient use of nature's bounty. In the end, none of Carver's products took off: neither his peanut-based makeup, nor his sweet potato rubber, nor his soybean paints and stains.

Carver was a longtime soybean fan, becoming very interested in this legume's possibilities in the early 1920s. As with the peanut and the sweet potato, some of his research on the soybean was in a branch of chemistry devoted to the industrial use of crops, called chemurgy, beginning in the mid-1930s.

Soybeans. The scientific name: *Glycine max*. In addition to paints and stains, Carver made oil, cheeses, flours, and coffees, among other foods, from this legume.

Carver and other chemurgists were keen on grains, vegetables, and fruits replacing petroleum as the basis for paints and other products, most especially fuel. "I believe the Great Creator has put oil and ores on this earth to give us a breathing spell," Carver contended. "As we exhaust them, we must be prepared to fall back on our farms, which is God's true storehouse and can never be exhausted." He was convinced that "every human need" could be met by "things that grow."

By the late 1930s, Carver was in poor health. Now in his seventies, he no longer taught. Speaking engagements were rare. One of his few research projects was on the healing properties of a favorite childhood fruit, the persimmon.

Carver spent most of the strength he had left laying the groundwork for an institution he hoped the future could use: the George Washington Carver Foundation. Its mission: to promote agricultural research by providing scholarships for science-minded youths and creating a museum of artifacts from Carver's life.

March 31, 1939: Carver chats with President Franklin Delano Roosevelt at Tuskegee during Roosevelt's trip through the South. Carver had sent the polio-stricken president a bottle of his peanut massage oil, believing his formula could revitalize withered limbs.

The easily fatigued Wizard of Tuskegee put up thirty thousand dollars as seed money for his foundation. During his forty-plus years at the school, he had spent very little of his salary and saved everything—even string. From things he had, he made almost everything he wanted, including clothing and paints.

Carver received mail from around the world. Some people wanted cures for troubled crops and consultations on infantile paralysis. Others wanted to let him know what an inspiration he was. His many honors include election as a Fellow of Britain's Royal Society for the Encouragement of the Arts, Manufactures, and Commerce (1916); the National Association for the Advancement of Colored People's Spingarn Medal (1923); and the Theodore Roosevelt Medal for Outstanding Contribution to Southern Agriculture (1939).

When Tuskegee Institute's George Washington Carver Museum was completed in November 1941, it contained a wonderland of agricultural, geological, and mycological specimens. Some seventy of Carver's paintings were also on view in a room of their own. Of this art gallery, *Time* magazine reported: "Visitors, impressed by the simple realism and tidy workmanship of the pictures, found still more to admire in the adjoining collection of handicrafts (embroideries on burlap, ornaments made of chicken feathers, seed and colored peanut necklaces, woven textiles) which the almost incredibly versatile Carver had turned out between scientific experiment and painting."

Carver's output ceased after he slipped and fell on a patch of ice while entering his museum in December 1942. On January 5, 1943, he died, though he probably would have disagreed with that word and said that he had merely ascended into the arms of his Great Creator.

Carver usually began
his day with an
early-morning walk,
specimen case in hand.
He always had a touch
of nature in his lapel.

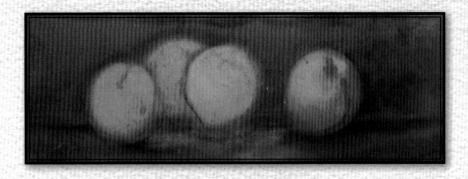

~ Afterword ~

Within six months of Carver's death, and with President Franklin Roosevelt's blessing, the U.S. Congress passed legislation for the creation of the George Washington Carver National Monument, a huge park in Diamond, Missouri—the first national monument for someone who was not a U.S. president. Carver's likeness would be on a postage stamp and, paired with Booker T. Washington's, on a commemorative half dollar. Soon a number of schools, libraries, college buildings, organizations, and even a submarine would bear Carver's name. All in praise of "the Peanut Man."

Carver's legacy came under fire in time. Some people thought him unworthy of praise because, like Booker T. Washington, he rejected open protest of segregation. They charged that whites intent on blacks remaining second-class citizens made Carver famous precisely because he was seen as a "non-threatening Negro."

Even while Carver lived, some scientists regarded him as irrelevant because when he was asked to detail his processes for plant by-products he talked more about revelations from the Great Creator than about scientific formulas.

Carver's detractors miss the man's ultimate and enduring value. People who care about the environment—who champion earth-care initiatives, from recycling to greater use of renewable resources—do not.

Carver's painting *Peaches*, made with Alabama clay–derived paint. Date unknown.

Notes

Opposite title page: "[E]ach . . . great whole." Carver, quoted in *George Washington Carver: Scientist and Symbol*, p. 38.

Page 3:   "I am . . . on" and "God's little workshop." Carver, quoted in *George Washington Carver: Scientist and Symbol*, p. 290, p. 268.

Page 8:   "I wanted . . . life." Carver, quoted in *George Washington Carver: Scientist and Symbol*, p. 18.

Page 9:   "considered foolishness" and "waste time on flowers." Carver, "1897 or thereabouts," in *George Washington Carver: In His Own Words*, p. 20.

Page 10: "You . . . little learning." Mariah Watkins, quoted in *George Washington Carver*, VHS.

Page 13: "We . . . no Negroes." Highland University official, quoted in *Carver of Tuskegee*, p. 20.

Page 18: Washington's letter to Carver. Reprinted in *George Washington Carver: His Life and Faith in His Own Words*, pp. 24–25.

Page 20: "[T]he acres . . . people." Carver, quoted in *George Washington Carver: For His Time and Ours*, p. 18.

Page 21: "The soil . . . grow?" and "I'll . . . I can." Washington and Carver, quoted in *Carver of Tuskegee*, pp. 34, 35.

Page 22: "the man . . . down." Carver, quoted in *George Washington Carver: In His Own Words*, p. 102.

Page 24: "The farmer . . . way." Carver, "Being Kind to the Soil," reprinted at www.stewardshipmandate.com.

Page 27: "Save . . . you want." Carver, quoted in "Black Leonardo," *Time* magazine, November 24, 1941. Accessed at www.time.com.

Page 30: "The Wizard of Tuskegee." Booker T. Washington had also been called that.

Page 30: "You'd . . . potatoes," and "No...work." Carver, quoted in *George Washington Carver: For His Time and Ours*, pp. 137, 138.

Page 31: Quotes and information from Carver's testimony. *George Washington Carver: In His Own Words*, pp. 103–13.

Page 32: "In dirt is life." Carver, quoted in *Carver: A Great Soul*, p. 45.

Page 34: "I believe . . . spell," "As we . . . exhausted," "every human need," and "things that grow." Carver, quoted in *George Washington Carver: For His Time and Ours*, pp. 66–67.

Page 36: "Visitors . . . and painting." "Black Leonardo," *Time* magazine, November 24, 1941. Accessed at www.time.com.

Selected Sources

Burchard, Peter Duncan. *Carver: A Great Soul*. Fairfax, CA: Serpent Wise, 1998.

——, principal investigator. *George Washington Carver: For His Time and Ours*. Diamond, MO: George Washington Carver National Monument, National Park Service, 2005. Posted at home.nps.gov/applications/parks/gwca/ppdocuments/Special History Study.pdf.

Carver, George Washington. Bulletin nos. 26, 31, 36, 38, and 43: *When, What, and How to Can and Preserve Fruits and Vegetables in the Home; How the Farmer Can Save His Sweet Potatoes and Ways of Preparing Them for the Table* (4th ed.); *How to Grow the Peanut and 105 Ways of Preparing It for Human Consumption* (7th ed.); *How to Grow the Tomato and 115 Ways to Prepare It for the Table* (2nd ed.); and *Nature's Garden for Victory and Peace*. Reprints. Eastern National Park and Monument Association, 1983–85.

Edwards, Ethel. *Carver of Tuskegee*. Privately printed, 1976.

Elliott, Lawrence. *George Washington Carver: The Man Who Overcame*. Englewood Cliffs, NJ: Prentice-Hall, 1966.

Federer, William J. *George Washington Carver: His Life and Faith in His Own Words*. St. Louis, MO: Amerisearch, 2002.

Harlan, Louis R. *Booker T. Washington: The Making of a Black Leader, 1856–1901*. New York: Oxford University Press, 1975.

——. *Booker T. Washington: The Wizard of Tuskegee, 1901–1915*. New York: Oxford University Press, 1986.

Holt, Rackham. *George Washington Carver: An American Biography*. Garden City, NY: Doubleday, 1950.

Kaw Valley Media. *George Washington Carver*. VHS. Shawnee, KS: Kaw Valley Films, 1984.

Kremer, Gary R., ed. *George Washington Carver: In His Own Words*. Columbia, MO: University of Missouri Press, 1991.

Mackintosh, Barry. "George Washington Carver: The Making of a Myth," *Journal of Southern History*, November 1976.

McMurry, Linda O. *George Washington Carver: Scientist and Symbol*. New York: Oxford University Press, 1982.

Merritt, Raleigh H. *From Captivity to Fame; or, The Life of George Washington Carver* (1929). Electronic edition at http://docsouth.unc.edu/neh/merritt.

Modern Marvels, George Washington Carver Tech. DVD. A&E Television Networks, 2005.

Perry, John. *Unshakable Faith: Booker T. Washington and George Washington Carver*. Sisters, OR: Multnomah Publishers, 1999.

Thrasher, Max Bennett. *Tuskegee: Its Story and Its Work* (1901). Reprint. New York: Negro Universities Press, 1969.

Washington, Booker T. *Up from Slavery* (1901). Reprint in *Up from Slavery by Booker T. Washington and Other Early Black Narratives*. The New York Public Library's Collector's Edition. New York: Doubleday, 1998.

~❧ Illustration Credits ❧~

Many of the archival images are reproductions of previously printed material as the originals are no longer available.

Bridgeman Art Library/David David Gallery, Philadelphia, PA, USA/"Southern Plantation" (oil on canvas), by Walker, William Aiken (1838–1921): front cover (top right), 4 (top); Brown Brothers: front cover (lower left), 21, 30 (left), 31, 34; Corbis: 13; George Washington Carver National Monument/National Park Service: front cover (left), 5 (right), 10, 11, 12; Image Research Team/Deborah Van Kirk: 28; Iowa State University Library/Special Collections Department: 15, 17; Library of Congress: 20, 23, 29; Courtesy of Merriam-Webster Inc.: 6; Courtesy of the Missouri State Archives: 8; National Archives and Records Administration: 35; North Wind Picture Archives: front cover (lower right), 30 (right); Courtesy of Simpson College Archives: 14; Tuskegee Institute National Historic Site/National Park Service: 7, 9, 18, 19, 24, 27, 33, 38; Tuskegee University Archives/Museum: front cover (center), (right), (top left), back cover, title page, 2, 5 (left), 16, 22, 25 (bottom), 25 (top), 26, 32, 36, 37.

~❧ Acknowledgments ❧~

Ever-growing gratitude to my editor, Howard Reeves, and the entire Abrams family. This is number five. Here's hoping for more.

To the fine folks at The Field Museum, Chicago—Laura Sadler, Senior Vice President of Museum Enterprises; Robin Groesbeck, Director of Exhibitions; Alice Kamps and Franck Mercurio, Exhibition Developers; Hilary Hansen, Project Manager; Lori Breslauer, External Affairs; Deborah Van Kirk and Jacque E. Day, Image Research Team—many thanks for a wonderful iron-sharpening-iron experience.

Thanks are also due to Peter Duncan Burchard, a great soul, for being so generous with information and insight; Teresa Valencia and Shirley Baxter at the Tuskegee National Historic Site for help with identifying some of the visuals; Curtis Gregory at the George Washington Carver National Monument in Diamond, Missouri, for his help searching for and scanning images; cousin Ondra Krouse Dismukes, who grew up in Tuskegee, for a close, thoughtful reading of an early draft; and cousin Frances Krouse, a retired Tuskegee University professor, for a miscellany of help. —Tonya Bolden

This book has been published alongside the exhibition *George Washington Carver* that was created by The Field Museum, Chicago, in collaboration with Tuskegee University and The National Park Service.

Lead Sponsor is The Motorola Foundation. Sara Lee Foundation is the Major Sponsor.

Library of Congress Cataloging-in-Publication Data
Bolden, Tonya.
George Washington Carver / Tonya Bolden.
p. cm.
ISBN 978-0-8109-9366-2 (Harry N. Abrams)
1. Carver, George Washington, 1864?–1943—Juvenile literature. 2. African American agriculturists—
Biography—Juvenile literature. 3. Agriculturists—United States—Biography—Juvenile literature. I. Title.

S417.C3B65 2008
630.92—dc22
[B]
2007028069

Book design by Maria T. Middleton

Printed and bound in China
10 9 8 7 6 5

Abrams Books for Young Readers are available at special discounts when purchased in quantity for premiums
and promotions as well as fundraising or educational use. Special editions can also be created to specification.
For details, contact specialmarkets@abramsbooks.com or the address below.

ABRAMS
THE ART OF BOOKS SINCE 1949

115 West 18th Street
New York, NY 10011
www.abramsbooks.com

The Field
Museum